GOTTFRIED FINGER

The Music for Solo Viol

edited by Robert Rawson and Petr Wagner

CONTENTS

Preface

Introduction ii
Sources v
Critical Commentary vi
Bibliography ix

Music for Solo Viol

1	Aria et Variationes in D major	1
2	Sonata in D minor	3
3	Divisions in G minor	7
4	Balletti Scordati	11
5	Sonatina in A Major	18
6	Sonata Prima	22
7	Sonata Seconda	26
8	Sonata Terza	32
9	Sonata Quarta	37
10	Sonata Quinta	42
11	Sonata Sesta	50
12	Prelude in E minor	55

Appendix

Balletti Scordati: Gavotte Double 56

Page-turns. Whilst every attempt has been made to lay out both score and parts with practical page-turns, we recognise that players may want to have extra loose pages for ease of performance. Photocopying for this purpose is permitted (with the obvious proviso that normal copyright must be respected), but players are welcome to apply to the publishers for a PDF file of such pages, which they can print out for themselves, and which we are happy to email to them at no charge.

ISBN 1 978 1 898131 22 9 2nd Edition © 2009   Fretwork Editions, London. General Editors: Bill Hunt & Julia Hodgson
16 Teddington Park Road, Teddington, Middx TW11 8ND, UK. (+44) 208 977 0924; mobile (+44) 7717 474263
www.fretworkpublishing.co.uk   fretworkpublishing@me.com

Dedicated to the memory of Petr Wagner
(1969-2019)
Alas too soon retir'd

INTRODUCTION

Since the time when what might be termed an 'early music revival' gained momentum in the twentieth century, Finger's music has primarily been associated with his many simple and tuneful pieces directed at the market for amateur recorder players. One of the main obstacles to a better understanding of his output has been the lack of many original sources. The problem was apparent early on; even in the eighteenth century Burney commented that Finger's sonatas were a 'polished but feeble imitation of Bassani or Torelli', despite the fact that Finger's music bears little resemblance to the music of either composer. In addition to the problems with early sources, many have been satisfied to pass comment on Finger's music without looking at it in much detail. This edition hopes to take an import step towards rectifying the matter by making available to players and scholars all of the surviving music for solo viol by Gottfried Finger — most of it for the first time.

Curiously, Finger never published any solo viol music, but rather he seems to have kept it for his own performance. Unlike much of the music he published for the amateur music market, his music for the viol is often very personal and emotionally exaggerated, ranging from the musing and mournful to the folksy and exuberant dance-like music of his native Moravia. Finger's viol music reveals an informed and ambitious musical mind with a tendency to include and reuse both his own ideas as well as folk songs and popular arias. Olomouc, the place of his birth, must have remained close to his heart since, among several other pseudonyms, Finger used "Msr Hannak", a reference to the Haná region around Olomouc.

Finger's music for viol is typical of the so-called Austro-Bohemian style, exemplified in the violin music of Schmelzer and Biber, among others. A common feature is the sort of patchwork design where the sections are sewn together by the ends of one section cadencing into the beginning of the next. Another prominent device is the opening flourish for the soloist over a drone bass, such as opens sonatas *Prima* and *Seconda* as well as the D minor *Sonata* — a hallmark of the so-called *stylus phantasticus*.

Biography

Gottfried Finger was born into a vibrant musical tradition in Olomouc in Moravia following a turbulent period in the region's history. The Czech historian Bohumír Dlabač (1758–1820) writes that Finger came from Silesia, but the composer's own Opus 1 (London: 1688) bears the inscription 'Authore Godifrido Finger, Olmutio Moravo' [sic]. Despite the long held assumption of some scholars that Finger was born c.1660, he must have been born sometime in the early to mid 1650s, since his music was already found in the hands of local scribes in Moravia by the early 1670s. It is from the Bishop's music collection at Kroměříž that the earliest pieces by Finger are preserved. He was almost certainly a viol player in the famous musical ensemble of Bishop Liechtenstein-Castelcorno and Finger's music for the viol reveals the influence of that court's formidable viol and violin virtuoso Heinrich Biber (1644–1704).

Finger probably arrived in London in the mid 1680s. By 1687 he was a member of the Catholic Chapel Royal — one of the most prestigious musical ensembles in the country. The competition for such a position must have been immense, and in the preface of his Opus 1 (London: 1688) Finger provides some insight in his address to James II (here translated from the Latin):

> Please excuse me that I dare to dedicate my works, whatever they may be, to such a ruler, the fame of whose rule, bounteousness, and generosity, which has spread beyond the frontiers of Britain everywhere throughout the World, has caused me to say farewell to the borders of my homeland, in order that I would expend all my enthusiasm and all the work which I have put together with great pains over very many years for Him. He has often presented himself as a common father, not only to his own people, but also to people of other nations.
>
> Therefore I declare that my sole ambition is that this music serves the Chapel Royal. Therefore if it would be granted to me to attach the name of the King to this work as the safest protection against those donkeys and petty critics, at this I would have satisfied the greatest of my desires, and would have been lucky to obtain what others are often accustomed to seek by loquacious and importunate canvassing, but in vain.
>
> SS: Your Majesties
> humble and obedient servant,
> Godefridus Finger

Finger did not follow James II into exile in 1688, but remained in London and started an impressive freelance career, composing music for over thirty-five stage productions, including operas, masques, instrumental suites, songs, dialogues and choruses. In 1690 he published *Six Sonatas or Solos* (three for violin and three for recorder) — the first set of pieces for solo instrument and continuo ever to be published in Britain. In 1695 he wrote an ode 'Weep ye Muses' on the sudden death of Henry Purcell and in the same year he was appointed to teach the viol at the proposed (but then later abandoned) Royal Academy of Music. When considering the pool of viol virtuosos from which to choose, Finger was chosen above stiff competition.

Finger's success in England came to an unpleasant end when he came fourth in a competition in 1701 (the 'Prize Musick') to identify the best opera composer in London, where each contestant set Congreve's libretto on 'The Judgement of Paris'. The winner was the nineteen-year-old John Weldon, followed by John Eccles, Daniel Purcell and Finger. According to Roger North, Finger was disgusted by the outcome of the contest and declared that

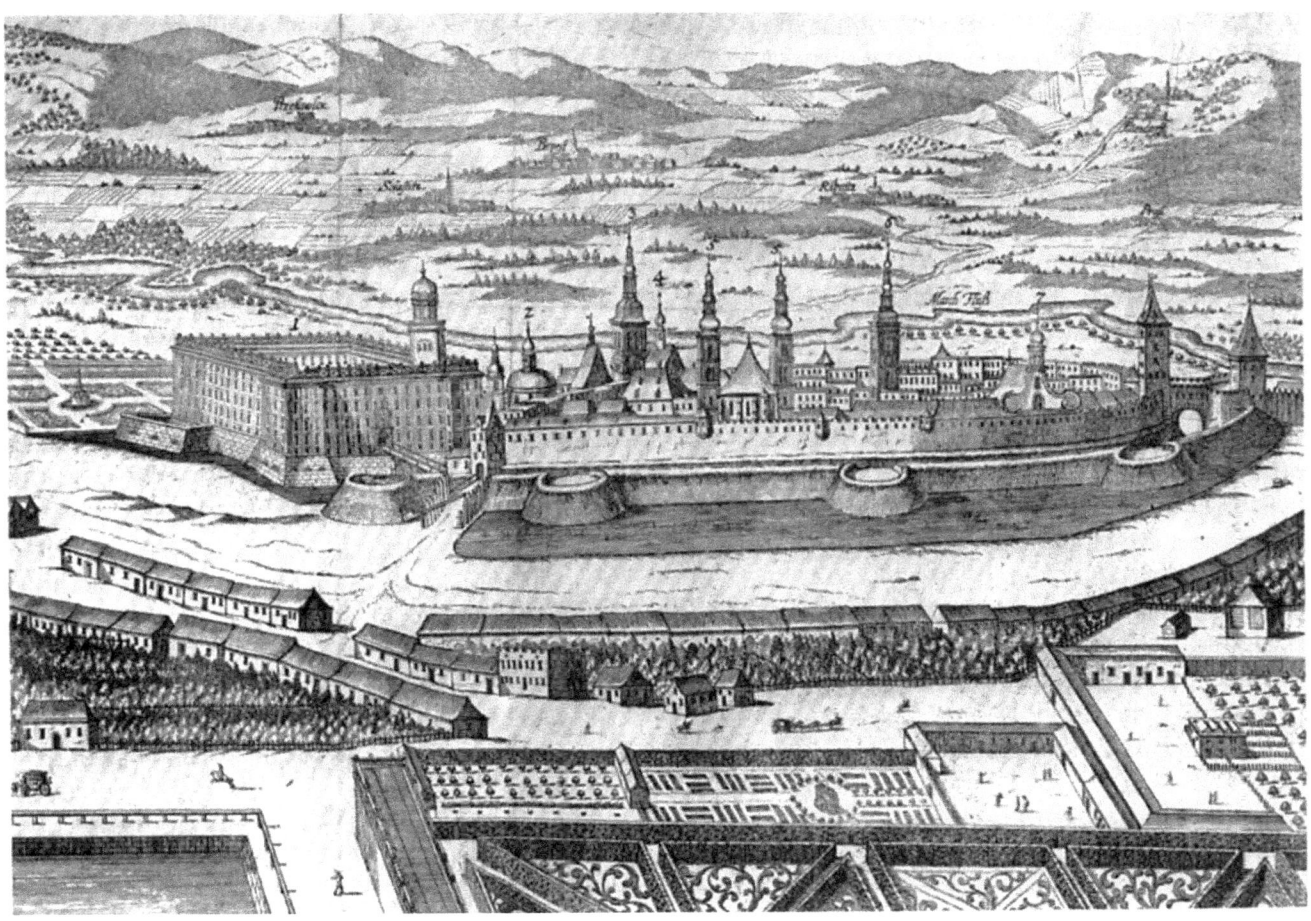

Engraving of Kroměříž in Moravia made by Justus van den Nypoort, after 1690. Note the Bishop's palace on the left, where the *Aria et Variationes* survives in autograph manuscript and was probably first performed.

'he was to be judged by men and not by boys and thereupon left England for good'.[1] In recounting the story later in the century, Oxford music professor Charles Burney (who himself travelled to the Czech lands in a famous account) declared that Finger was 'perhaps the best musician among the four'.[2] Finger's music for England continued to be reprinted and performed for decades after his return to the continent.

Finger arrived in Vienna later in 1701 where he was apparently trying to further his opera career. George Stepney, the British envoy in Vienna reported that, despite feeling that the Duke of Somerset has been partial to Eccles and Weldon, Finger planned to perform Eccles's setting 'The Judgement of Paris' in Vienna (surely the first performance of English opera on the continent). Stepney wrote home to Lord Halifax:

I thank you for your Eccles his Musick, w[hi]ch. I suppose is got by this time to Hamburgh and will shortly be here, where Finger will see it performed to ye best advantage; He assures me notwithstanding the partiality which was shown by ye Duke of Somersett and others in favour of Welding and Eccles, Mr. Purcell's Musick was the best (I mean after his own, for no Decision can destroy the Love we have for ourselves).[3]

The next two decades were busy and productive, but almost no music survives from this time. In 1702 he was in Berlin in the service of the Queen of Prussia, Sophie Charlotte where one of his performances was seen by Telemann; and by 1705 he was in Wrocław (Breslau) in the service of Duke Karl Philipp of

---

1 Roger North, *Roger North on Music, Being a Selection from his Essays from the Years c.1695–1728*, ed. John Wilson (London: Novello, 1959), 354.

2 Charles Burney, *A General History of Music, From the Earliest Ages to the Present Period*, 4 vols. (London: for the author, 1776–1789; reprint, F. C. Mercer, London: G. T. Foulis & Co., 1935), 934.

3 Philip H. Highfill Jr., Kalman A. Burnim and Edward A. Langhans, *A Bibliographical Dictionary of Actors, Actresses, Musicians, Dancers, Managers, and Other Stage Personnel in London, 1660–1800*, vol. V (Carbondale: Southern Illinois Press, 1976).

Neuberg, the younger brother of the Elector Palatine. He remained in Karl Philipp's service for the rest of his life. In 1707 he was a Kammermusiker in the Innsbruck Hofkapelle and rose to the position of Konzertmeister in 1708. He seems to have maintained this post when he followed the court to Neuberg an der Donau in 1717, to Heidelberg in 1718, and to Mannheim in 1720 where his expertise in handling a variety of instrumental forces helped lay the foundations for what would become the 'Mannheim school' made famous under Stamitz.

Throughout this later period Finger continued to travel widely and rub shoulders with many prominent composers of the age. Telemann saw him in Berlin; he collaborated with, among others, Johann David Heinichen (1683–1729), Jean Baptiste Volumier (c.1670–1728), Augustin Stricker (died after 1720, Bach's predecessor at Cöthen); and on several occasions acted as joint godparent to the children of chapel musicians with Attilio Ariosti (1666–1729). The breadth and scope of Finger's output is astonishing; he composed hundreds of works for a variety of instrumental permutations (often in pioneering ways), composed numerous comedies, dramas, singspiels and operas in English, Italian and German, and probably visited every important European musical centre of his day. His name last appears on the court records in Mannheim in 1723 and he was buried there on 31 August, 1730.

The Continuo Parts

Identifying music by Finger has been a difficult task at times, since he often deliberately obscured his identity. In the 1960s the pioneering work by Arthur Marshall on Finger's viol music identified an otherwise anonymous set of six viol sonatas, and in doing so found two of the otherwise missing continuo parts. For the sonatas *Prima*, *Seconda, Terza* and *Sesta* we have had to reconstruct them. The theme of the *Sonata Terza* is identical to one used in a trio sonata by Finger preserved in Brussels, and to our delight the continuo part fitted the opening section of the viol sonata. The piece presented here as *Balletti scordati* has no title at all in the manuscript, nor does the opening movement, but we have adopted the title from the common convention found at Kroměříž and an *Intrada* is found as the opening movement in other similar works by Finger and his contemporaries. Likewise, there is no title on the autograph manuscript for the divisions in D (Aria et Variationes). For those pieces without titles in the sources, we have retained those that we used on a recent recording of most of these pieces.[4]

Acknowledgements

We are grateful to the Bodleian Library, Durham Cathedral Library and the Archbishopric of Olomouc for permission to consult, transcribe and publish the music in this edition. We would like to express special thanks to Jan Krejča for his contribution in the preparation of the continuo parts, particularly leading up to the recording of some of the pieces in this collection, and also to Peter Holman for numerous helpful suggestions and especially for identifying Lully's 'Scocca pur' as the basis of the G minor Divisions.

Robert Rawson and Petr Wagner
April 2009

---

4 Ensemble Tourbillon Petr Wagner, "Sonatae, Balletti scordati, Aria et variationes," (Prague: Arta, 2005).

THE SOURCES

Czech Republic

A *CZ-KRa* A 4679. Parts (1): 'viola di gamba'. Single sheet, upright folio, 32 x 21 cm; copied after 1670, autograph. Attribution based on (1) Finger's autograph, and (2) the composer's later use of this melody in other viol pieces. [Divisions]: 'Adagio' [Key: D]. This work was only recently discovered, having been identified in the late 1990s, based on the handwriting (autograph) and the fact that it contains a theme that must have been among Finger's favourites. Like many sets of divisions, the continuo does not survive, but is easily reconstructed by simply following the chords in the viol in the later variations (particularly bars 41–44). This is probably the earliest solo piece by Finger to survive and is the work of an ambitious teenager.

Great Britain

B *GB-Ob* Mus. Sch. C.61. Parts (1–2). WM: foolscap (resembles Heawood 2002) on inside front cover: 'Divisions for the bass violl, Decemb. 3d Anno Domini 1687'; on inside back cover: 'Given to F. Withy by his Schollar Henry Knight of Wadham College, 4 Dec. 1687', Finger division copied around 1692: pp. 56–57, [no. 37, divisions] 'G. F.',Vdg, bc [Key: g]. These Finger divisions are in the hand of F. Withy and the book (presumably blank) was given to him in December 1687, however the nearest dated piece in the manuscript is 1692 and the Finger divisions were probably copied about around that time.

C: *Ob* Mus. Sch. D.228. Parts (2): [2 Vdg]. Oblong folio, 24.2 x 29.5 cm. This bound volume was once a collection of loose folios, which were apparently bound together based on size and content in the nineteenth century — though the Finger materials are all closely related. Solo viol pieces used in this edition: ff. 99v–100r, 'Sonata Prima', Vdg solo [Key: D; no. 6 in this edition]; ff. 100v–101r, 'Sonata Seconda', Vdg solo [Key: D; no. 7 in this edition]; ff. 101v–102r, 'Sonata Terza', Vdg solo [Key: A; no. 8 in this edition]; ff. 102v–103r, 'Sonata Quarta', Vdg solo [Key: d; no. 9 in this edition]; ff.103v–104r, 'Sonata Quinta', Vdg solo [Key: Bb scordatura; no.10 in this edition]; ff. 104v–105r, 'Sonata Sesta', Vdg solo [Key: a; no. 11 in this edition]. This relevant section of this manuscript (see above) contains a set of six anonymous, sequentially-numbered sonatas with continuo (though the continuo parts for numbers four and five also survive in D. 249, see below). The entire D.228 MS was bound together in the second half of the nineteenth century and it was not until Arthur Marhsall's research in the 1960s, when he discovered the D.249 concordances, that Finger was identified as their author — and not until the late 1990s that the manuscript was identified as an autograph.[5] It would seem that the manuscript was copied in the 1690s, but it is unclear where. Certainly the sonatas *Quarta* and *Quinta* borrow heavily from earlier works, when Finger was still in Moravia. The opening theme of Sonata Quarta is from his *Sonata Augustiniana* for two bass viols (D-SÜN) and the fast arpeggiated section of the *Sonata Quinta* was borrowed from the prelude of Suite no. 3 for barytom and viola da gamba. There is marked stylistic difference between (at least some of) these sonatas and Finger's much earlier work. Sonatas *Prima*, *Seconda* and *Quinta*, however, are in the mould of the Austro-Bohemian style, most closely associated with Heinrich Biber. The watermark on the paper is not English and may be Italian. It could be that Finger actually copied this manuscript in Italy in the hope of securing a position there; this might also account for the highly Italianate quality of those sonatas not based on earlier material. Until more source material comes to light, this will remain speculation.

D *Ob* Mus. Sch. D.249. Parts (2–4). Upright folio, 30.8 x 26.4 cm. Music for viols and violins largely from the collection of James Sherard, who seems to have copied the music from and with Finger. ff. 42v–44r, 'Sonatina' [Key: A; item no. 5 in this edition], parts (2): viola di gamba [and bc], hand of Sherard; ff. 55–57, [Sonata in D minor, no. 2 in this edition], hand of Finger; ff. 134–137, 'Mr Finger viola di gamba solo' [Key: d] no. 9 in this edition], parts (2) viola di gamba, cembalo, hand of Sherard; ff. 142–145, [Balletti discordati; Key: A; no. 4 in this edition], parts (2), [vdg, bc], hand of Sherard; ff. 153–156, 'Sonatina Mr Finger' [Key: B flat/A; no. 10 in this edition] parts (2): [vdg, bc], hand of Sherard. The *Balletti scordati* is untitled and unattributed in the manuscript, but is here attributed to Finger on the basis of style, tuning and its relationship to other pieces in the manuscript with it, which are certainly by Finger. This manuscript also contains sources, in two parts (Vdg and bc), for the sonatas Quarta and Quinta in D.228, the latter is ascribed here to 'Mr Finger'.

E *DRc* A27. Score. Music for solo viola da gamba with and without continuo. Oblong folio, 21.9 x 28.5 cm; 173 ff. Copyist: Philip Falle (1656–1742): f. 123r, 'Prelude Mr Finger' [Key: e].[6] The Prelude in E minor is the only solo viol piece by Finger in the large and diverse manuscript collection of the viol-playing Canon of Durham Cathedral, Prebendery Philip Falle. This short piece is one of Finger's most English pieces for solo viol. very similar is style and duration to preludes of Simpson, William Young and other English violists. For that tradition it would probably not have had a continuo part.

---

5 Arthur Marshall, "The Viola da Gamba Music of Godfrey Finger," *Chelys* 1 (1969). For the identification of Finger's autograph see Robert Rawson, "From Olomouc to London: the Early Music of Gottfried Finger (c.1655–1730)" (Royal Holloway, University of London, 2002), 30–36

6 For details of this fascinating manuscript see Margaret Urquhart, "Prebendary Philip Falle (1696–1742) and the Durham Bass Viol Manuscript A27," *Chelys* 5 (1973–4).

CRITICAL COMMENTARY

Editorial Procedure

1. In all pieces except the two in scordatura tuning (see Note 2 following) accidentals are modernised and apply for the duration of the bar unless cancelled. In the Basso Continuo figuring, however, the original practice is maintained: naturals are not used.
2. All editorial or cautionary accidentals are given in brackets, and their duration is the same as in (1) above. This includes those used to interpret the notational conventions of the period with regard to accidentals, namely that they generally apply only to the note to which they are attached and therefore require cancellation in modern notational practice.
In the two scordatura pieces (4. Balletti Scordati and 10. Sonata Quinta), a different policy is adopted, due to the unusual nature of the scordatura notation system used by Finger. He uses the 'grip notation' typical of the Austro-Bohemian school (such as Biber) rather than the tablature of the English lyra-viol school, but the result is much more difficult to interpret; indeed, it may even be deliberately obscure, with the object of excluding those who have not been initiated into its mysteries. Accidentals in this edition generally follow the 17th century practice described above, their duration being only for the note to which they apply. But where, within the bar, the same pitch is immediately repeated, or a figure is repeated (which may itself contain pitch repetitions) the first accidental applies to all following iterations (see for example 10. Sonata Quinta bar 4, where the original notates all 3 e flats). However, more cautionary' accidentals have been added elsewhere in order to clarify issues which arise from the notation system. Rather than overload the text with editorial intervention, a supplement published with this edition includes a version of each piece in tablature, to resolve several inherent ambiguities.
3. All editorial ties and slurs are given in dashed lines.
4. Barlines have been regularised without comment. In dance movements, double barlines have been replaced with repeat barlines, except where indicated.
5. Basso continuo figures are given as they appear in the source(s), but have been standardised.
6. Some continuo figures have been added without comment if their necessity is made clear by the surviving parts (for example, 4–3 suspensions).
7. The continuo symbol ♯ appearing on its own in the sources has been transliterated as ♯3 in cases where confusion might arise.
8. For those pieces with long, sustained continuo notes to support running passage-work in the viol, editorial ties have been added. Note, however, that these ties are inconsistently applied in other sources of similar repertoire. Whilst an organ can sustain without difficulty, Frescobaldi comments that such long notes can be restruck as required when performed on the harpsichord
9. In the tables of variants, pitch is indicated by the Helmholtz system (c' = middle C); symbols are numbered from the beginning of a bar (the end of a tied note counting as 1).
10. All alphanumeric references ('RI') refer to the complete catalogue of Finger's music (see Rawson, 2002)
Abbreviations: sbr = semibreve; mn = minim; cr = crotchet; qu = quaver; squ = semiquaver; dsqu = demisemiquaver

1 Aria et Variationes in D major (RI-16)

A: *CZ-KRa* A4679

The set of variations in D major is one of Finger's earliest surviving works and it is based on a melody that Finger would revisit many times (also heard in the *Sonatina* in A and in the *Sonata Seconda*). The variations reveal a remarkable level of virtuosity as well as early evidence of Finger's trademark writing for the viol: melodic *cantelena* in the highest register of the instrument, thick-textured and guitar-like chordal writing as well as rapid arpeggiation throughout the range of the instrument

bar	part	item(s)	comment
15	Vdg	7	f"
26	Vdg	8	a
34	Vdg	5	a
36	Vdg		MS has [music], the notes in brackets crossed out.
40	Vdg		MS has [music], the notes in brackets crossed out and final cr changed into a mn
52	Vdg		The original notation of this bar is shown in the upper stave, but it seems questionable in view of the crossings out in bar 36 and 40. An editorial alternative is shown in the lower stave.

2 Sonata in D minor (RI-147)

D: *GB-Ob* Mus. Sch. ff. 55–57 (autograph).

This piece was copied by Finger, probably in England, sometime in the 1690s. There is no author attributed in this manuscript. The sonata was published in a version for violin (Sonata 1, Sonatiniae XII, Vienna and Frankfurt, 1692) by the Italian violinist and composer Ignazio Albertini, who was working in Vienna around the same time Finger was at Olomouc and Kroměříž. It would seem that Albertini's set of sonatas was in circulation well before the deceased composer's brother published it in 1692. However, the Finger version was copied before Albertini's was published; of course Finger had every opportunity to know the pieces as a young man — they are listed in the 17th-century Kroměříž inventory. On the face of it, the most logical explanation is that Finger made an arrangement of the violin sonata (a common practice amongst viol players at the time), but there are several sections in Albertini's version that are not present in the Finger version. Nevertheless, even if the original work is by Albertini, Finger's version contains enough idiomatic adaptation to warrant inclusion here as a separate work.

bar	part	item(s)	comment
12	Vdg		final chord is qu
110	Vdg		no fermata

3 Divisions in G minor (RI-140)

B: *Ob* Mus. Sch. C.61, pp. 56–57 (hand of F. Withy).

This set of divisions from the early 1690s suggests that Frances Withy (c.1645–1727) might have studied (however informally) with Finger. Although the ground appears to follow the typical passacaglia pattern, the cadence at the end reveals a different source. This ground was particularly popular in England at the end of the seventeenth century and is based on Lully's Italian air 'Scocca pur'.[7] A number of short passages have numbers indicating the notes of a scale ('1, 2, 3, 4', etc.) The original manuscript may be incomplete — it ends with custodes for a G minor chord, which could be shorthand indication for the final chord of the piece or perhaps indicate that there were once further divisions.

The symbol of four dots (bars 36, 37 & 38) could indicate an ornament; similar signs are found in this sort of context in 17th century English division music for viols to denote such ornaments as 'backfall' or elevation'.[8] However, the symbol is used elsewhere in the MS of the this piece merely to indicate the start of a new set of variations out of sequence (a sort of *nota bene*), so its use in these bars remains unclear.

The tempo marking at the variation beginning in bar 96 is an editorial suggestion, influenced by similar instances in the violin music of Schmelzer and Bertali (the latter's sole surviving violin sonata was copied by Finger) where some treacherous passagework is accompanied by instructions to slow down and the resume tempo on the next variation. A good and appropriate example is found in the case of Bertali's *Ciacona* [sic] for violin and continuo (*CZ-KRa* A883) where just such a passage is marked *adagio adagio* and the next variation marked *batutte col pulso* — the latter instruction strongly implying that the *adagio adagio* indicates a slower and more free tempo and that the following section resumes the earlier tactus.

bar	part	item(s)	comment
1	Vdg/bc		Time signature omitted
1	bc	1	fermata
13	Vdg	1	no accidental
51			four-dot symbol before system
65	Vdg	1	no accidental on e'
69	Vdg	1	no accidental on f
85	Vdg	2	no accidental
86			four-dot symbol before system
86	Vdg		notated 9/6
96	Vdg	8	clef change is after note 8, corrected to follow 5
103	Vdg	1	no accidental

4 Balletti Scordati (RI-149)

D: *Ob* Mus. Sch. D.249, ff. 142–145 (hand of James Sherard)

The *Balletti scordaturi* is typical of the *sonata da camera* of Biber, Schmelzer and other central-European composers; and the opening *Intrada* strongly suggests these origins. Another Austro-Bohemian trait is the use of *scordatura*, by which the player de-tunes certain strings of the instrument but reads the staff notation as if he were playing in normal tuning. While this requires some mental gymnastics, the result is a beautiful and resonant sonority. Unlike Biber, Finger was much more in tune with the French style and this suite is a testament to his absorption of certain French dances and traits. There is a curious feature in the slow penultimate movement, where the grave and serious mood is interrupted by a rather rowdy folk dance (*presto*), as if a group of revelling peasants had stumbled into a sombre courtly gathering — such juxtapositions often caught the imagination of central European composers (such as Schmelzer's *Dudelsack* sonata and Biber's *Die Bauern kirchfahrt gennant*).

Cautionary accidentals: in addition to those outlined in the Editorial Policy (see above) a large number have been added in the solo part to instances of the note b' (semitone above 7th fret, 1st string). In every case, b' flat is clearly intended but no flat is notated in the MS; no comment has been added.

bar	part	item(s)	comment
Allamande			
12	VdG	7	notated squ f, squ a
14	VdG	7	notated squ f, squ a
Sarabande			
21			In both the solo and BC parts there is only a single barline between bars 20 & 21, with a double bar following bar 21. In the BC part (only) "2ᵈ" is written above bar 21. This is interpreted to indicate that bar 21 is intended as a reverence chord.
Double			
	bc		The Double part is not written out separately, but the Sarabande part is followed by an instruction to repeat.
2	Vdg	6	notated c
Gavotte			
	BC		The words '3 times' above first stave
1	Vdg		in 2nd & 4th chords the lower note is notated e'
Aria			
	Vdg		no time signature; tempo instruction in bc only
8	bc	2	figuring has ♭4; similarly following bar
9	bc	2	no accidental
15	Vdg	5	no accidental
16	Vdg	12	no accidental
17			tempo instruction in bc only
			in both parts there is a repeat indication into bar 18; bar 20 into 21 has a normal double bar
28	bc		no 'petite reprise' indication
Gigue			
4	Vdg	1	notated e' natural, which arguably lies better under the hand; but the advantage seems to be outweighed by problematic harmonic consequences
20	Vdg	5	no accidental
23	Vdg	3	no accidental

---

7 See Klakowich, Robert. "'Scocca pur': Genesis of an English Ground." JRMA 116, no. 1 (1991): 36–77.
8 See for example divisions by Jenkins in Royal College of Music MS921, as published in Fretwork Editions, *Duos for two Bass Viols and Continuo* ed. Andrew Ashbee, Vol.1 (London 2002) and Vol.2 (London 2005)

5 Sonatina in A Major (RI-142)

D: *Ob* Mus. Sch. D.249, ff. 42v–44r (hand of Sherard)

Although anonymous in the manuscript, this attractive piece is very similar to other works by Finger — especially the opening theme that he uses so often. This tunefully elegant and Italianate piece is typical of Finger's more mature style and is probably from his English period. After settling in England the Italian influences become stronger than the French ones that characterised much of his earlier work. The final chaconne is a good example of this. Rather than the hair-raising virtuosity of his earlier chaconnes, this one is stately and well balanced with a greater concern for development of motif than for dazzling his audience.

bar	part	item(s)	comment
92-3			the MS has double bars marking each subsequent reiteration of the ground, but there is not one here. It is likely that each 5-bar section is intended to be repeated.

6 Sonata Prima (RI-145)

C: *Ob* Mus. Sch. D.228, ff. 99v–100r (autograph)

The opening section of this sonata features two virtuoso flourishes over long pedals (one tonic, one dominant) each interrupted by melodic adagios that feature some colourful chordal writing. This is followed by a contrasting Italianate allegro, similar to sections of some of Finger's violin sonatas, with some lighthearted, yet demanding passagework. A short triple-time section precedes another that mirrors the opening of the sonata. Here two shorter flourishes over pedals (this time dominant, then tonic) intersperse lyrical, slurred passages, before cadencing into a short gigue-like conclusion.

bar	part	item(s)	comment
18	Vdg	11	no accidental
137-8	Vdg		slurs written too ambiguously to be sure what grouping is intended (likewise 143–4)

7 Sonata Seconda (RI-146)

C: *Ob* Mus. Sch. D.228, ff. 100v–101r (autograph)

The opening flourish over a tonic pedal in the *Sonata Seconda* is very similar to the one at the start of the *Sonata Prima* (a stock in trade device of the Austro-Bohemian style) and owes much to the violin sonatas of Biber. This is followed by short and lyrical adagios that are repeatedly interrupted by effusive and virtuosic passagework. The ensuing aria with variations in one of Finger's favourite tunes and can be found in two other pieces in the present collection. A somewhat agitated and melancholy adagio follows in the relative minor, only for the brightness of the opening bars to return for the two final triple-time dance-like sections.

8 Sonata Terza (RI-141)

C: *Ob* Mus. Sch. D.228, ff. 101v–102r (autograph)

This piece marks a noticeable departure in style from the first two sonatas of the group and follows the sonata da chiesa layout. It is also interesting to note that it borrows the opening theme from another work by Finger, a trio sonata for two violins and continuo in a manuscript in Brussels (*B-Bc* 24910, ff. 8r–8v), a factor which helped in composing the otherwise missing continuo part. This is a bright and athletic work and one of Finger's most 'Corellian' sonatas for solo instrument and continuo. There are two passages of descending notes under a slur (bars 69 and 76: Example 1) with dashes between the slur and the notes. They are represented in the present edition with a dash for each note, but the intention of the composer is open to interpretation. It could be that Finger intended each note to be gently articulated with the wrist under a single bow stroke (as suggested by Simpson). It is also possible that the marks are to indicate an equal rhythmic performance of the notes under the slur.

Example 1: *GB-Ob* Mus. Sch. D.228, Sonata Terza, detail, (bar 69)

bar	part	item(s)	comment
60	Vdg	1	missing alto clef

9 Sonata Quarta (RI-148)

C: *Ob* Mus. Sch. D.228, ff. 102v–103r (autograph)
D: *Ob* Mus. Sch. D.249, ff. 134–137 (hand of Sherard)

This opening movement of this sonata is a re-working of a theme from an earlier work, *Sonata Augustinia*, for two bass viols (*D-SÜN* MS 12). The transformation reveals something of Finger's change in style from that of his early works, so heavily indebted to the much freer Austro-Bohemian style, to the more structurally controlled Italian style that he later championed in England. The conclusion of the sonata features a short passage for continuo alone, which would become something of a trademark in Finger's English-period sonatas. In compositional terms, it may be Finger's finest bass viol sonata.

bar	part	item(s)	comment
8	bc	4	figure is 6 without sharp (D)
32	Vdg		tempo indication missing in solo part(C,D), taken from bc (likewise bars 79, 111 and 130)
43	Vdg	7	no accidental on b (C,D)
45	Vdg	4	lower voice cr e not notated (C)
48-52	Vdg		no ties (C)
48	bc	4	no accidental (D)
59	bc		all the 7,6 figures in this bar and the following are written 6,7 (D)
84	Vdg		no slur (C)
99	Vdg		no slur (C)
105	Vdg		no 'piano' marking (D)
118-9	Vdg		no slurs (C)
121	bc		figures 4,3 are written 3,4 (D)
123-4	Vdg		no slurs (C)
126-7	Vdg		no slurs (C)
135	Vdg		no slur (C)

bar	part	item(s)	comment
142	Vdg		no slur (C)
142	bc		2nd figure is 3
148	Vdg		no slur (C)
			chord notated dotted sbr (D)

10 Sonata Quinta (RI-144)

C: *Ob* Mus. Sch. D.228, ff. 103v–104r (autograph)
D: *Ob* Mus. Sch. D.249, ff. 153–156 (hand of Sherard)

This is the second of the six sonatas in D.228 that has a surviving continuo part. The A major scordatura used in this sonata is identical to that used in a number of other Finger works (such as the *Balletti Scordati* published here), but the continuo part from D. 249 is in B flat. It would seem that there is a good reason for this and that is because the B flat tuning allows the player to leave the top D string at pitch (where most of the melodic material is) and retune the lower strings which are primarily employed for chordal playing. For reasons of convenience (for example, if one wanted to programme other pieces using the A-major scordatura) we have also included a continuo part in A. There are no tempo indications for this sonata in D.228 and all of them are taken from D. 249.

This sonata features a demanding *arpeggiato* section (bars 63–80) that is very similar to a passage in an earlier suite for baryton and viola da gamba (*D-SÜN* MS 12).[9] There are also similarities to some works by Marais and even much later composers like Abel. It is likely that the small noteheads indicate notes that should be fingered in the left hand, but not necessarily be bowed. Marin Marais wanted similar notes to be held in the left hand for sympathetic vibration, though Roland Marais later argued that these small notes could sometimes be played by the bow as well. There are several possible bowing solutions to this passage. The notation suggests using separate bows, but slurred bowing could be added at the player's discretion. The latter suggestion is not made explicit in the notation, so performers must decide for themselves.

Cautionary accidentals: in addition to those outlined in the Editorial Policy (see above) a large number have been added in the solo part to instances of the note b' (semitone above 7th fret, 1st string). In every case, b' flat is clearly intended but no flat is notated in the MS; no comment has been added.

In several places the notation is confusing — and might be considered erroneous, were it not that the sources agree — in that the intended sounding pitch is sometimes written instead of the correct scordatura instruction. This variation of practice does not follow a coherent system. Rather than obscure the original text with multiple alterations, an asterisk is placed above the notes concerned and a comment below seeks to clarify the issue with a graphic illustration.

bar	part	item(s)	comment
6	Vdg	2	no accidental (D)
7	Vdg	6	c sharp notated d flat (D)
8	Vdg	1	scordatura should logically read:
9	Vdg	2	(3rd cr beat) scordatura should logically read:
10	Vdg	1	both here and on a similar chord in bar 24, the sounding notes of the Eflat chord (albeit, omitting the necessary flats) are written instead of the scordatura notes. It is a simple *barré* on the 5th fret and should logically read:
11	Vdg	2-3	similar issue to bar 8.1 (see above):
13	Vdg	12	qu rest in place of chord (D)
15	Vdg	3	no sharp on f (C)
16	Vdg	1	no sharp on f (C)
16	Vdg	3	no sharp on f (C)
18	Vdg	4	no accidental (C)
22	Vdg	1	accidental only in (C)
22-3	Vdg		the notational principle here seems to be that notes on the 2nd string up to the 6th fret are written in scordatura, but from the 7th fret upwards are notated as sounding pitches. Confusingly, it apparently does not to apply to the 3rd string, whose note on the downbeat of bar 23 ought under this system, to be notated at its sounding pitch of c'
23	Vdg	2	notated f' (D)
23	bc	1-2	4-3 figures above C in MS (D)
24	Vdg	5	3rd cr beat: see comment bar 10 above
33	Vdg	6	notated sharp (D)
42	Vdg	7	no accidental (C, D)
45	Vdg		here and in the following bars see comment to bar 22 above
47	Vdg	1-2	sharp signs against e' (D)
52	Vdg	1	mn g' notated a' (C, D)
52	Vdg	1-2	cr f', cr e' notated g', f' respectively (C, D)
53	Vdg	1	no accidental on g (D)
58	Vdg	1-2	notated c' sharp (D)
63	Vdg		second half-bar: no small noteheads (C)
63-5			these three bars repeated, presumably a copying oversight (C)
64	Vdg		each f in 2nd half-bar: no sharp (C, D)
64	bc	1	figure (sharp sign) on 4th qu beat, & not on 1st
65	Vdg	2	each f in 1st half-bar: no sharp (D)
67	Vdg	1	notated with additional stem down (D)
69	Vdg	1	no accidental (C)
69	Vdg	2	no accidental (C, D)
	Vdg		second half-bar: no small noteheads (C)
			this 4th fret *barré* should logically be notated:
70	Vdg		second half-bar: no small noteheads (C)
73	Vdg	14-6	chord does not change on 4th qu (D)
74	Vdg	1	this 5th fret *barré* should logically be notated:

---

9   Robert Rawson, "Gottfried Finger and the Baryton," in Festschrift Alfred Lessing (2003), ed. Bernard R. Appel and Johannes Boer (Düsseldorf: Foundation for Historical Performance Practice, 2003), 53-61.

bar	part	item(s)	comment
74	Vdg	17	this 7th fret *barré* should logically be notated: (but see note to bars 22–3)
74	bc	1	no accidental
75	bc		3rd cr beat: no accidental
77	Vdg	14-7	chord does not change on 4th qu (D)

Aria

bar	part	item(s)	comment
8-9			no ⫼ (D)
12	Vdg	3	these chords should logically be notated:
13	Vdg	1	no sharp on f (C)

Double

bar	part	item(s)	comment
1			⫼ between the Aria and Double (C)
1	bc		no mention of Double in the MS continuo part, so this edition has repeated both the bassline and its figures from the Aria
6	Vdg	1,3	notated flat (C)
7	Vdg	15	no sharp (C)
8-9			no ⫼ (D)
9	Vdg	15	notated c' sharp (D)
13	Vdg	1	notated flat (C)

11 Sonata Sesta (RI-143)

C: *Ob* Mus. Sch. D.228, ff. 104v-105r (autograph)

The Sonata Sesta is probably one of Finger's most restrained works, revealing clearer structures and simpler medelodic invention. The opening thematic material evolves rather organically from a rising a-minor triad, and the lucidity and vigour of the first section of the work is contrasted with the rather odd chromatic and rhetorical slow movent. It has some structural similarites to the clearly defined sections of the *Sonata Terza*, and reveals strong Italian influences in terms of form. The long passages of running semiquavers are evidence of the newer Italian style championed by Corelli.

bar	part	item(s)	comment
19	Vdg	2	e', assumed to be copyist error
127			A repeat of each section is probably intended, but none is notated.

12 Prelude in E minor (RI-15)

E: *DRc* A27, f. 123r (hand of Philip Falle)

The solo prelude in E minor is probably one of the latest works presented here and may have formed part of a lost suite. It shows the influences of English preludes for the viol, by Simpson and Young in particular, and it has an improvisatory flow about it. Unlike the sonatas published in this present collection, this sort of prelude would not have had a continuo part. An attribution on the last system reads "Mr Godfrey Fingher".

bar	part	item(s)	comment
17	Vdg	9	The meaning of the ornament sign here and at the end of bar 18 is uncertain, but is probably a form of trill. (A similar sign is used by the English virginalists).

Appendix

Balletti Scordati: Gavotte Double

D: *Ob* Mus. Sch. D.249, f. 142v (hand of Sherard)

This piece is crossed out in the MS. There is a harmonic problem in bar 10, first crotchet beat, where the Gavotte bass does not fit with the solo part, and has been altered in the edition.

bar	part	item(s)	comment
8	Vdg	1	sharp

Bibliograpy

Burney, Charles. *A General History of Music, From the Earliest Ages to the Present Period*. 4 vols. London: for the author, 1776–1789. Reprint, F. C. Mercer, London: G. T. Foulis & Co., 1935.

Marshall, Arthur. "The Viola da Gamba Music of Godfrey Finger." Chelys 1 (1969): 16–26.

North, Roger. *Roger North on Music, Being a Selection from his Essays from the Years c.1695–1728*. Edited by John Wilson. London: Novello, 1959.

Highfill, Philip H. Jr., Burnim, Kalman A. and Langhans, Edward A. *A Bibliographical Dictionary of Actors, Actresses, Musicians, Dancers, Managers, and Other Stage Personnel in London, 1660–1800*. Vol. V. Carbondate: Southern Illinois Press, 1976.

Rawson, Robert. "From Olomouc to London: the Early Music of Gottfried Finger (c.1655–1730)." Royal Holloway, University of London, 2002.

— "Gottfried Finger and the Baryton." In Festschrift Alfred Lessing (2000), edited by Bernard R. Appel and Johannes Boer, 53–61. Düsseldorf: Foundation for Historical Performance Practice, 2003.

Urquhart, Margaret. "Prebendary Philip Falle (1696–1742) and the Durham Bass Viol Manuscript A27." Chelys 5 (1973–4): 7–20.

CD Recording

Petr Wagner, Ensemble Tourbillon. "Sonatae, Balletti scordati, Aria et variationes." CD recording. Prague: Arta, 2005.

1. [Aria et variationes]

* Basso Continuo part editorially reconstructed

©2009 Fretwork Editions FE28: Gottfried Finger, The Music for Solo Viol, edited by Robert Rawson & Petr Wagner

2. [Sonata]

Finger/Albertini?

3. [Divisions]

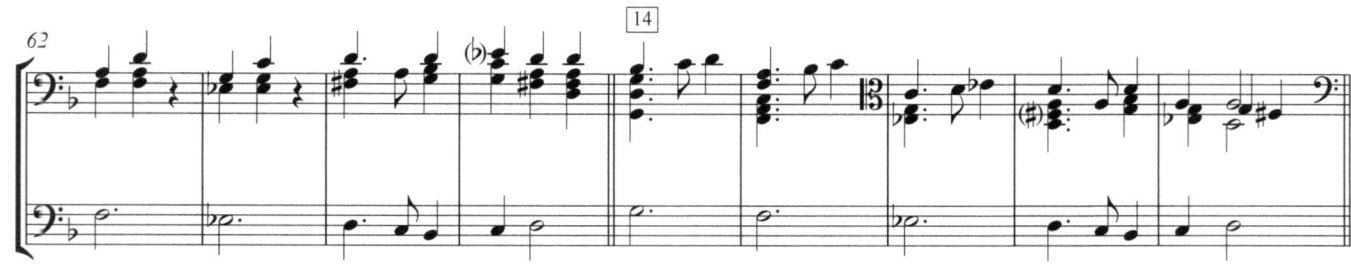

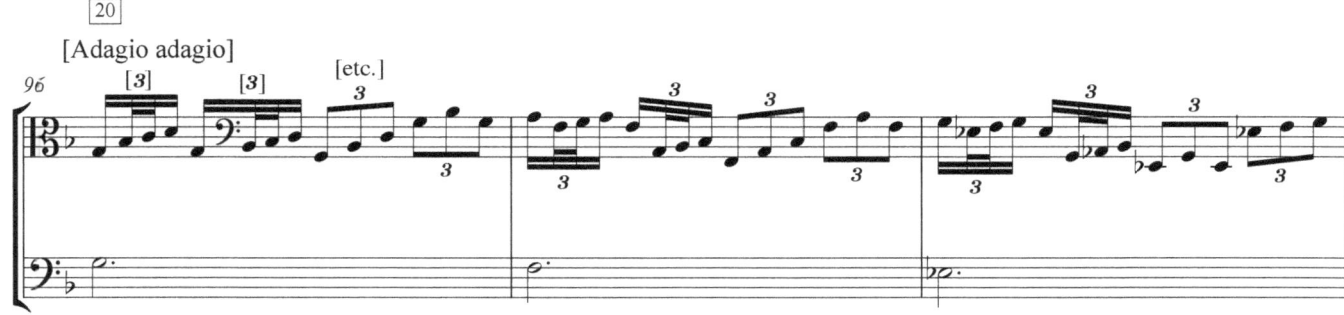

4. [Balletti Scordati]

[Intrada]

Allamande

Courante

Sarabande

Double

[petite reprise] [last time]

Gavotte

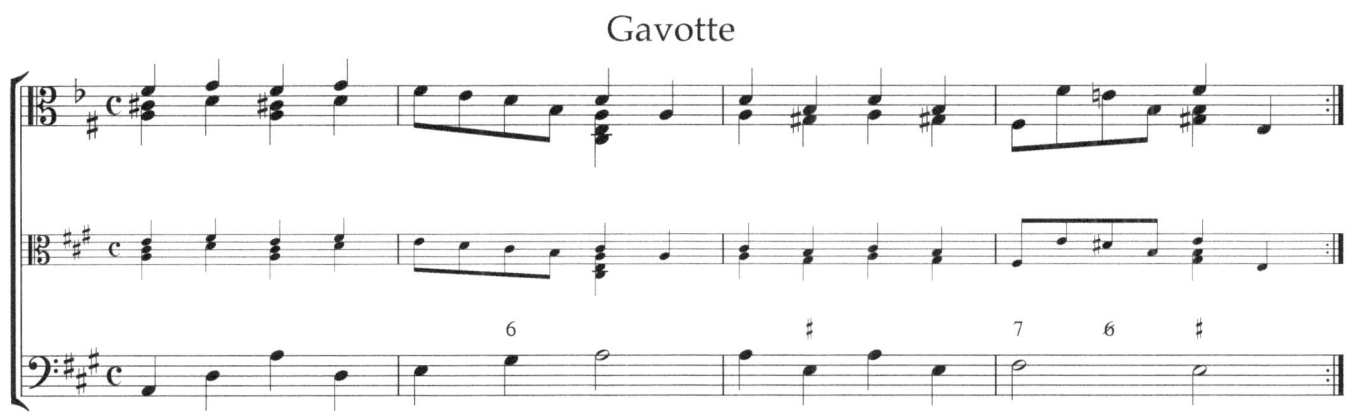

5. Sonatina

* See Commentary

6. Sonata Prima

*Basso Continuo part editorially reconstructed

7. Sonata Seconda

* Bass Continuo part editorially reconstructed

©2009 Fretwork Editions FE28: Gottfried Finger, The Music for Solo Viol, edited by Robert Rawson & Petr Wagner

8. Sonata Terza

* Bass Continuo part editorially reconstructed

This page is left blank in order to minimise page-turns

9. Sonata Quarta

10. Sonata Quinta †

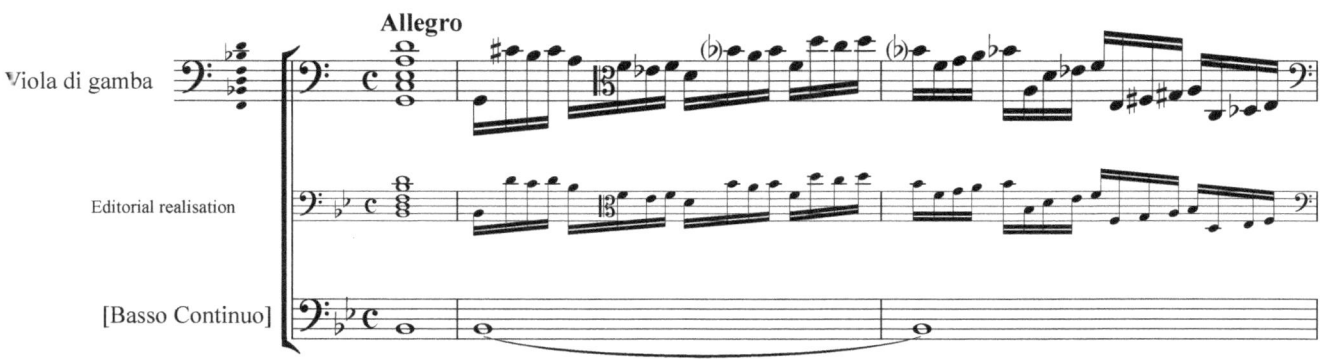

† A transposed score (into A, for pairing with piece 4. Balletti Scordati) may be found in the Supplementary Material
* See Commentary for this and other chords similarly indicated

©2009 Fretwork Editions FE28: Gottfried Finger, The Music for Solo Viol, edited by Robert Rawson & Petr Wagner

Aria

Double

11. Sonata Sesta

* Basso Continuo part editorially reconstructed

12. Prelude

[Viola da Gamba]

APPENDIX

4. [Balletti Scordati]

Gavotte: Double

[Basso Continuo]

www.ingramcontent.com/pod-product-compliance
Lightning Source LLC
Chambersburg PA
CBHW0=2017090526
44588CB00024B/2890